Yam

by Carl M. Polaski

illustrations by Roberta Collier-Morales

Harcourt Brace & Company

Orlando Atlanta Austin Boston San Francisco Chicago Dallas New York Toronto London

Mom and Dad went out.

Fred had to sit with Pam.

Fred played with Pam.
Then he said, "Now you
go to bed."

3

Pam hid. Fred was mad.
"You are a bad little
fox!" he said.

"Yam jam!" said Pam.
"Mix it! Fix it! I will not
go to bed until I have
yam jam!"

Fred got six yams.

**Fred mixed and fixed
yam jam for Pam.**

Did Pam go to bed?

No! <u>Fred</u> did!